Here and the Water

Here and the Water

SARAH COLES

Gomer

First published in Wales in 2012 by
Gomer Press, Llandysul, Ceredigion, SA44 4JL

ISBN 978 1 84851 483 6
A CIP record for this title is available from the British Library.

This book is published with the financial support of the
Welsh Books Council.

Printed and bound in Wales at
Gomer Press, Llandysul, Ceredigion

To my girls
Emily, Megan and Evie

Acknowledgements

Many thanks to Nigel Jenkins and Stevie Davies for their unfailing generosity and wise words. Thanks also to Tracey Fitzgerald, Patrick Chapman, Jo Furber, Peter Thabit Jones, David Oprava, Ira Lightman, Lucy, Joe, Bethan and all at The Crunch for support and encouragement. Acknowledgements to David Hughes for 'Ambition is Critical'. Much love to Peter Williams and Patricia Borley.

Contents

Cwm Ivy to Whiteford Point

This path is no more ours than the air
that swoops the coarse, green marsh-grass grey
and salts the stunted blackberries,
gathered in grubby fistfuls
by children's nonetheless hands.

Ring down, running seaward, beyond
the broadleaf-bordered land, through pines,
hushing in foreign whispers that carry
no further than themselves.

Shush down, dapple-shouldered, along the borrowed path –
a foothold between land and land –
until it loses itself, in a grand, vacant gesture,
to the broad-swept bay that flies
with the low rushing of fast-blown sand.

The curve of the beach, smooth as a hipbone,
pockets only wind. The sea
can keep its treasures for milder shores.
Here, the air is dead of echo; distilled of ghosts
that drift from the rust-rivet lighthouse,
standing half-submerged by water
and creaked with silhouetted birds.

All the better . . .

I think that you are dangerous. I see
my downfall in the sideways of your smile;
hear my quickened breath hiding
in the dark, brown depth
of your voice –
foreign, yet familiar.

How could you have found my path?
I'd hidden it with brambles
and masked its scent with hyacinths
that pushed cleanly through
the moist, mushroomed humus
of the forest floor.
How could you have known

that I taste copper in my mouth
when you speak my name
and when the breeze lifts your soft hair,
to glimpse white skin beneath?
I didn't say that you could walk with me
and yet, you are here, striding
at my left side, laughing
at your own green-flashing tales
that buzz my skin with nettles.
If I turn

and face you –
stand still in the quiet of the pine-dead air
and let my guard fall slowly
down from my shoulders –
will I see your true form?
Will my tired eyes be witness
to another painful metamorphosis?

I am no little girl lost
and these silver strands
are not moonbeams in my hair.
I think that you are dangerous
but just as scared as I am.
Take my hand. The forest is dark
and the canopy is birdless.

Rattus Rattus

We, too have our stories.
Ours are the stories of the hidden places.
We etch them on the gutters
and tell them softly with our footfalls in the eaves.
Their telling is a whisper below earshot
and their reading is in spaces between words.

They are also your stories.
We share your history and we have leafed,
scratch-footed through your pages,
inscribing our tales
between the columns of your scriptures.
Our bodies have brushed
the drying ink on scroll and parchment
and from the rise and fall of empires,
to the floorboard-creaking cradle song,
we have slept amongst the breaths and commas,
in the hidden spaces.

Our stories are your stories.
We were there at your beginning
and thronged in your shadows
as you strode out of Africa
and as you peopled drifting continents,
we rejoiced in your resourcefulness.

Ganesh.
Allah.
Yahweh.

Through your provision, we have become legion
and still our numbers rise,
even to the edges of the frozen axis
of the turning world.

Our stories are your stories.
They tell of movement and displacement,
of persecution, poisoning
and the taking of the children into the hill.
Because your provision is not without its price,
we show you not our faces uncovered,
and take darkness as our veils.

We pray among your dispossessed,
inscribing our thanks
between the print-stains of your newspapers
that fly, windswept in the Underground
or cover fevered bodies in shop doorways.

London.
New York.
Delhi.

We live amongst your fallen
and we live amongst your kings.

Morning

Morning settles on the garden with the benign, wet smile of a holy idiot, brushing chilly dew onto bare footsoles grubbed by the unswept path. It rests soft elbows on the garden fence, tracing cobwebs with a lazy finger. It says that I can take it if I want it. I pretend not to notice and light a cigarette.

Earth-smells of morning
fade beneath my exhaled smoke –
morning coughs but smiles.

The garden is greener with rain and all is swollen in the sea-mist; door and gate and eyelid saturated stubborn. It would take a month of sunshine to draw out all the moisture – make them fit again, but it's too late now. It's autumn already.

Glistening fenceposts
suck up rain-shared memories
of being a tree.

Inside the house, the air too is moistened by the laundry and last night's words, which condense in rivulets against the cold of the window pane. Your breath, now lingering in liquid, sticks folds of greying net onto the glass as it creeps downward, stitch by stitch. I wonder how long your presence will circulate the microclimate of the house now that you're gone.

Morning sky opens
in blue and flashing fork-tail –
last of the swallows.

Yan Tan Tethera

You three
golden sheaves,
glossy leaves,
wolf cubs, lambs,
each face a kaleidoscope
of he
and me
and the thousands who have made us.
You run along sand like you don't know;

heedless of the dead
beneath your soft soles and go
about your shellfish-worrying ways,
pulling tightly on the thread that
fed you in the dark, warm space.

Yan, Tan, Tethera,
three heads,
one dark, one fair,
one red, each
bowed and poring
over small, wet worlds
as you crouch in parlance with the bay,
each at a distance further away
and it's only perspective –
the thread of an eyeline,
but it stops the breath in my throat
just for a moment.

Evie

Sleep then, you –
wax-cheeked kernel of night.
Sleep, youngest of three –
accident of last-ditch love.
I will not hope
anything for you. My hopes
are tired and predictable.

The night is not velvet
and the barn owl's screech
as distant as the fading cries
of poor, banished Lilith.

I cannot give you all
the hills and bays of our land
and hold them steady for your running
or have the pebbled streams
brim with sunshine for your laughter

but hope and fear are wed
under the laws of tide and moon,
inseparable by jealous gods,

so sleep as your mother watches you
with the gift of her not hoping.

Elvers

It would be our last summer here.
The long-shadow heat of the late June evening
gave us no warning –
drunk as we were with the opulence of tall grass
and trailing woodsmoke along the heavy, bough-dipped Wye.
We wove stories and fingers on the road from The Sloop
and laughed waspy cider-breath into the darkening sky.

At the bridge, low voices
and dipped torches
straightened our meander –
the glint of rifles amongst nets
quickening the night sober.

Worth more than gold,
these slivers of soft glass,
these gulf-riders from the Sargasso,
scooped out here in writhing, moon-glint netfuls.

Four thousand miles
to the mouth of the Severn,
gasping along mud banks,
or tangled, tide-lined on wet grass,
these legion strands of life had ridden
waves of inherited memory,
to fatten in the border rivers.

We found our path home by quiet moonlight –
careless and torchless as we were.
Soon our own internal rhythms would pull us
each along inconceivable distances.

Together

When autumn quietly declares itself,
it sends soft messengers to tell of its coming
– leaf-mould smells and mist-dabbed webs
on faintly echoed rag-and-bone mornings
that murmur into vague and muted days;
at once as close and as distant
from the summer's surly storms
and buzzing heat
as night from day:
always touching, yet with faces turned
towards their own concerns.

Hay Bluff

We took a drive out
at the start of winter.

We both knew it was over;
both stiffly aware
of our own faces' compositions,
second by second.
Our speech was small and strangled
and the children were quiet.

Heavy mist held the valley down
that day, making the ways unfamiliar.
We took high roads in bright, white sky,
until we breached the surface of the fog
and emerged into the blue of a clear, winter noon.

At the highest point, we stopped,
our breath condensing
on the insides of closed, cold windows.
We let the children run about the hillside.
They described small, concentric distances
while below us, the Shires and the Cwms
had disappeared beneath a new, thick landscape of cloud.

Digging Potatoes

Chough
Spade in stony earth.
Chough
Daddy digs potatoes.

Borage overgrown,
yellow eyed
and high as little red-hoody-head.

Purple star flowers;
white furred stems
and leaves that catch
beads of dew.

Y byd.
Duw.
Dyma'r dydd.

Chough

If you cut a
worm
in half
there are two
worms
and they follow each other
everywhere.

Daddy's soft, black hair
gently parts in the breeze
and he stoops and he digs
and there is a little laugh
in my stomach

Chough

but it's a laugh that feels like sadness too.
I know he's watching but I won't look up.
I know his round glasses
are glancing off morning sunlight
and the vapour of his breath
is silver-white,
dancing droplets round his head
but I must not look up
and break the perfection of his looking.

...

Chough

My girl; sitting with your back to me
in the newly dug earth.
All I can see is the round of your cheek
and your moleskin-brown soiled hands
and,
when you stretch out your arms
to shake the loose earth
from your sleeves,
your tiny, clean, white wrists.

Chough
Chough
Chough

The hazy
morning light is swimming
and I'm digging blindly –
slicing through potatoes.

Sketches

On Swansea Bay, a prison officer
puts a seashell to his ear
and holds it there, not noticing
that the sea is licking
his polished, leather shoes.

Behind Uplands Crescent, a florist
spoons cat-food from a tin
onto the potholed lane and the wind
parts the back of her brown hair,
betraying white roots.

In Brynmill Park, a small child
runs in the same direction
as the wind and scatters
the creaking ducks, which settle
again onto the black water.

At High Street Station, a young man
with no luggage steps
across the new-laid paving slabs.
Ambition is Critical.

5am

Night and morning touch here
and the skin between them,
thin as water membrane,
conduits nerves of soft light.

Each feels the contours and scars
of the other's little history
short as the mayfly's ephemera
of wings in fluttered union.

Night withdraws, still tasting
morning's luminescence
and sighs itself
into silent repose.

Miscarriage

No, keep your Sunday dress on.
We'll go for a drive, up to the lake
and I will tell you my plans for the garage.

You can look out of the window –
and I will keep the quiet curve of your cheek
in my peripheral vision.

Herd

Know that where you now stand or sit;
where you whittle away
the fading Sunday light;
where you shake sand from your hair
or gather up the day's high sun rays,
captured brittle yellow on folded newspaper;
where a tuneless whistle or the scraping
of a fork across a neighbour's plate
or the rattle of a magpie presses
the evening's quiet inward –
inward and further in –

know that here, they may have stopped
and approached the white bones
of their kin, arced in the receding grassland.
They would each have touched the ribs
in turn and passed the three-holed skull
between them and the light
would have been fading, as it is now.

Potter's Field

With the dwindling glow of the city at his back
and the daylong heat scuffed dusty
from the clay baked beneath his feet,
he thought nothing of the equinox –
the second tilting of the year
although the dry vine leaves
trickled by like ghosts of wine and water
and a harvest moon
thinned its rays on the path ahead.

Half a year ago, the springtime
and those very leaves in bud
had framed his only dying memory;
of voices in a garden; of hands and feet
and the taste of blood
on his swollen lip, that even now
he could not keep himself from biting.

But all else, before and after, was gone
and scarcely worth remembering –
a family, a son maybe, the clamour
of the net-strewn harbour,
the silver of the pouring tilapia
and laughter on the sea.
He would, himself, have had a childhood

but even a maternal,
stumble-sprung embrace, an olive-kiss,
a first taste of pomegranate juice
in the shade of the Cypresses
had become dust, blown by a prophecy
and he knew nothing of them now.
But he knew this field and knew also
the tree – the very branch
that would be strong enough to bear his rope.

Acting

I saw my daughters hanging redcurrants
by their yellow stalks
from the branches of a dusty, stunted laurel.
They called me to look
at the miracle of the dead tree,
alive again with berries.
I feigned surprise
and they suppressed their laughter;
gathering shining bowlfuls.

Translucent flesh, burst by small fingers,
or trodden under bare heels, bore
yellow seeds in threes and fours
huddled in scarlet pools.

The children pushed whole fistfuls
of these sour little fruits into their mouths
and counterfeited pleasure with their voices
but the bitterness of disappointment
is tricky to disguise on faces
expecting sweetness from beauty.

Beach House Remembered

She remembers it in white light
flickers of a cine-film –
soundless but for the whirr of memory;
sky blending into sea,
long hair blown across cheeks
and lips, stumbling with silent
laughter across pebbles.

Whitewashed and drifted
with wood and crisped bladder-wrack
to the door – itself stiffened with sea salt
and hung with threaded shells,
the beach house exists only here:
in the perfection of the visual memory.

She does not recall the sound of traffic
on the ocean road behind
nor the linger of woodsmoke and bitumen.

Open the door.
The rafters are clung
with the gourds
of deserted swallows' nests
and angled light falls
from the draughty roofspace
onto an empty room.

Phonetics

On a street in Wales,
builders load a van,
Dan,
dan, dan,
without a word.
dan dy rhyda danw
dan.
The sound
dan y derw
is like a sermon
dan y dedw
in an empty chapel.

Bethesda,
Jerusalem,
danw dan . . .

Gwion Lost

Small boy; too small, that hand,
trembling to thread a wooden bead
onto a shoelace or crayon-trace the curves
of an elusive 8 with tree-frog grip;

I should have guessed,
as Earth hurled itself towards
the far-point of its analemma;
as other children flew, like autumn leaves,
ringing the cold air ragged with their play;

I should have known, small boy,
that you would steal my year-brewed wisdom
with a suck of your thumb
and would leap from me as hare,
as trout, as swallow
over and under this many-backed land
and that your life, though toiled-for,
breath by small breath,
would be as short as four harvests.

I should have carried you, babbling,
to the water's break;
set you down in a black wave
where you could weave
your gurgled verse unheard
as you rolled with the shoals of dumb urchins
along the silence and the dark of the sea bed.

I should not have let your eyes
beguile my anger at your loss.

I should have pecked you up like a grain of wheat.

Phone call

She shivers tired limbs
and drenched with his words
she sighs as night gapes and keens
to the lonely sound
of cats fucking in the back lane.
She'd better wrap it up tight, this night
and tie it to the tiny knot in her stomach
that only he can unravel;
pushing his words inside her
until only her mouth and her throat are left dry.

Woodsmoke aches through a crack in the door
stuffing dried leaves
into the open mouths of corners
and she wonders if anyone ever died
from not being touched.

Tomorrow will be bright
and blue, autumn sky will
bleach the printed leaf-ghosts
from the concrete
as she sees the kids to school.
Heading home to smoke and sigh,
with last night's dishes piled high
in the back of her mind
she swears that this night
she'll unplug the phone,
but she always forgets.

Beach House

Night tide rolls the shingle westward
to the beach house door.

Moon-drift ghosts the blown glass frosty
and we, beneath the rat-paw quiet eaves
submerge in oyster bed
and breathe like fire under water
prising open mussel shells
and tasting seaweed, softly
with fronded tongues of anemone.

Drift-riding currents, we suspend time
in pools, deep green and brined
by our own saline skin.

By morning, our breath
has danced the window
into ice and we rise, blanketed,
shaking white salt from our hair,
to defy water with fire.

Back lanes

Weary of staid, front-door facades
and the conspiracy of neat, fenced lawns,
we walked home through the back lanes
in the midday shimmer

and saw the truth of every house
spilled out on linen-billowed washing lines:
house-ghosts meeting air and dust
blown north from the Sahara.

Our feet scuffed up low clouds
of cement dust from spectred
dandelion and chamomile.

We walked on and did not look back
at the diminishing perspective
of identical yards, lest the ghost-linens
should reach out to us
and petition us for meaning.

Sunday

Between my clasped, clean
Sunday morning hands, I as a child
would slyly peep
at my grandfather beside me as he knelt
and I'd listen to his great, deep chest
exchange the incensed air
for a week's worth of dark nickel fumes.
Wide and sallow veined, his cooper's hands
stood loosely palm to palm
and I would wonder how a man so strong
could fix his moistened eyes
on images of Mary and the Infant
and be tamed. But then
my thoughts would leap to the priest's
most welcome words to 'go in peace
to love and serve the Lord'
(which heralded my playtime)
so forgot the incense and the mystery
of my grandfather's hands;
then I and all my brothers owned the day
and burst the Sunday greyness
with our play until the sun was old
and made its slow and laboured
genuflection to the world
of the grass-green-handed children
of Sunday afternoon.

Spinning

A cloud-hung playground above the village
tips the slateland roofslides

up, down,

with the tilting axis of the see-saw, unbalanced
by the mismatched weights of children
whose voices carry only so far
into the lidded valley.

I spin my own girl on the spider's web –
wrapped as she is in the gossamer of cloud.
I spin her and her laughter
diminishes, returns,

diminishes as the sky gathers into a dark ball.
'I can't see what I'm looking at,'
she says.

Snow

Adrift in a small boat, lain
the full fathom of me,
bow to stern
and the fog knowing no more about water
than I do of flesh.

I could float on the narrow, snow-lined river
as it thaws;
prow churning grey slush
and leave a long wake of clear, black water –
mirror-flat and packed with stars.

Snow on the road,
on the bridge over the river;
snow on the field beyond and to the houses
and every human ear straining to believe
that it's the first to notice the bound silence
and the muted breeze.
How quiet the snow makes everything.

Snow on the rushes;
snow flanked on the banks, softening
ratholes to moon-scooped dents
and the silence here would be inertia –
just the drag behind the clamour of the usual;
the tail of an awaited comet
or a cold morning sky
herringboned with contrails.

Angel

Nothing's on the street but black cabs
passing, black against black
like raindrops on slate.
I've been sitting on the kerbside,
watching the angel
in the quiet of the cuspal moment
between too early and too late.
Trapped inside the telephone box,
his white wings beat
against the panes
like a moth in an upturned wineglass.
I should open the door
but the gravity of the half-divine
would drag me inside.
His eyes and wings wild, he would pull
at my hair, bruise my lips – his wingtips
dirtied with blood and cigarette ash.
I could only hold him.
What good would that do;
soft angel hair against my cheek;
coarse human hair against his neck
and the scent of heaven
in the dent behind his ear?
Hold him and hold him
until his wings fold slowly between his shoulders –
all silent but for our breathing and the hum
of the telephone dangling from the cord.

Watson, come here . . .

The Garden was reclaimed in sepia
and the ticking of significant clocks.
Dust rolled like tumbleweed
across scuffed footprints
and the Tigris and Euphrates
ran indigo with spilled ink.
Bell, Baird and Babbage
sat drinking cans of beer
amongst the ruins,
which bloomed with primroses
and the fruitless Tree
creaked and warbled,
heavy with Galapagos finches.

A wish

He made her a picture and called it 'A Wish'.
A bed – soft pastel folds and two inclined heads
hair roughed against custom-indented pillows
and a cascade of blankets.
So still – the sleep between
dream-sleeps portrayed by a few strokes
and the faint cheek-smudge blush
transferred by finger from the cinnabar quilt.
He would have drawn it at night,
while his wife and children slept,
then washed his soiled hands, watching
the colours' mingle trickle down the plughole.
He'd have padded back mildly
to the stale warmth of a too-solid sleeping shadow.
Maybe he posted it while walking his dog;
concealed it between domestic bills;
maybe he turned cold
as he heard it drop
into the letterbox,
but when she opened it, some days later,
the rusty pastel dust stained her dress
and the faces were unrecognisable smudges.

Pleuronectiform

Stoop down low on the sandbank,
look deep into the water, no,
focus now, better
still, lie across the width
of the narrow footbridge
and peer down,
like this:
still now. The river's over sand –
glimmers of broken mother
of pearl
look. There's one. No,
there. Look.
The warm seep of oil,
from the sleepers
reclaimed for this bridge
is not important,
nor is the rust there, staining your hands.
Keep still, keep quiet and look:
there – there
they're the colour of the sand
and you can only see them by their shadows,
in the sunlight after noon,
scudding from the shadow of your raised hand
into shadow.

From a well-wisher

She had a letter today
and read it under the apple tree,
the baby clasped to her breast,
and the older children playing further off
in the falling blossoms.

Waelisc

We call ourselves by a given name –
gently, maiden,
with the humility of unglazed
pottery – hard, brittle maybe
but porous to the colours
of grass and wine,
and sheened with much use by rough hands.
Not weathering so well, we are shaped
like our limestone coast
or the waterscored hills
but still we remain,
smooth-edged,
standing,
watching,
quietly defiant
as trees.

Colin and Janet

They were out again today,
the next-door neighbours,
planting bulbs for Spring.
They worked like separate parts
of one machine. Colin trowelled holes
in even spaces while Janet popped the bulbs in.
Later, they were sweeping up dead leaves,
well, Colin was, while Janet held the bag.
They both waved, when they saw me,
and I sneered,
(how cosy,
how twee,)
and thanked my luck I'm free
from the suffocating ritual of marriage
that makes people
into halves
and went inside to make a cup of tea.
One cup.
One teabag.
For one . . .

The Square

The village curls up at the edges into hills;
weighed down in the middle
by the bulk of chapel
and behind every house-front,
and by every sunken window,
sits a small, brittle uncle who is cradling his tea
in the valley of the blanket on his knees.

In the square in front of the dark, one-eyed chapel,
there's a child-scried ball
drawing arcs through the drizzle.
The girls clip clop
from the yellow of the chippy
and their laughter is lost
in the soft of the valley
that's cradling the clouds –
making dusk always early

and the brittle little uncles,
all sitting by the windows
tut tut at the children
as their cups and saucers rattle
in the blesséd woollen valleys
of the blankets on their knees.

Narcissus

I do not want your hours in my house,
nor your minutes carried clinking
from room to room
in that willow-patterned cup and saucer
with its balanced spoon.
I can no longer give countenance
to your days of late moons
and the wet chattering of starlings
in the trees behind the garden.
I can no more wake to weeks of frost
and the curled up fists
of oak leaves, to find
discarded half-hours of silent weeping
in pools around the kitchen
and on the bedroom floor.
There's no space here for scrunched-up months
dotted around the overflowing bin or clogging
up the sink with the coffee-dregs.
Once I watched a
fortnight unfold itself in dirty, dishpan water
and saw the detail of its veins and creases
as it rose and fell, riding small eddies
under my swimming reflection.

Cefn Sidan

The children called me and a fox ranged out,
on long-shadow legs, from between the dunes.
The emptying beach was all echoes now and footprints
like elipses of broken conversations.
My children too, were quiet. They knew
it was significant, somehow, to see a young fox
here and at such an aged time of day,
in eye-level light from the west.
But that was some months ago.
I don't know if they will remember it
as I do – as it really was:
sand dusting their arms and shoulders;
a hasty wind tugging at their hair.

After the Flood

The rooftops were drying in the morning sun.
Their facets were dulling from apex to gutter
and a hazy sea breeze
brought muttering gulls
to the quieted vertices of Constitution Hill.

Low tide lapped the doorsteps
of Hanover Street
and the city was gone.

Only the Guildhall clock
stood out above the water, still telling
the wrong time
on all four faces

and Sweyn's longboat met the swell
again, after a dry spell millennium-long.
I wondered if you had been one of those
who had rolled into the dark, or if you had gone,
amongst the light travellers,
the rapid-breathed hundreds,
to find higher ground.

Eleven

She will prick her finger . . .
She's slipping away from me
in red. That's her colour:
the colour of the embers
that she worries to death,
there on the dark bay,
with a branch of copper beech.
She will follow silence with silence . . .
She watches the sparks –
the tiny souls of flames
fly into the night.
She will weep at the beast's unmasking . . .
Once, she let a ladybird
settle on her hand. It scaled
her small, white finger
and crawled across her bitten nails.
Its rolled, black wings emerged
behind it like a tail –
the bright shell halved itself
and it was gone.
I could not console her with the rhyme
about the house-fire and the departed children.

Running

The cloud's shadow
ran over the hill and away.

It ran across the yellow hill
and was gone, before the child
could even push the blown hair from her face.

Visiting Hours

I got there just before the end
of visiting hours – brought you stolen
lilies from the cemetery
knowing you'd enjoy the joke
but more because the memory
of wickedness would stir
inside your lengthening dreams;
your pulse quickening audibly
in the stillness. You might be moved
by the long bubble-clung stems,
thickening, refracted under water,
pulling on the last of the oxygen
in the hospital vase. How many
offerings of flowers had gasped
their last in that plain vessel
during visiting hours? You'd have laughed
in your dark way but you were sleeping
and your wife was there, warm
and vacant and she held the flowers
on her lap with slow, heavy thanks.
We sat either side of your rises and falls
as she spoke of milligrams and hours
and so many measurements of space.
Her hands would gently, accidentally,
brush the petals as she talked.
I almost told her then
that we had never touched each other
but she smiled just as the bell
was sounded and looked down at her fingers,
stained yellow by the stamens and I knew
there was no need.

I'm sorry. There were no stolen flowers.
I never made it for one reason or another.
When I got the email, it had already been a fortnight.
I took my children down to the river where they fought
and made white paper boats.
It was true though:
we never touched each other.

D'cu

D'cu moves slowly through the hollyhocks,
deep in his own age; neck interred
in the collar of his greatcoat. Black
and white he is among butterflies,
tapping his stick upon the path ahead.
He is the oldest man in the square mile:
the others taken by the dust.
His shelves hold heavy books
and a Holmes Stereograph. He has seen
Ginza looking north; the Devil's Kettle;
the Grand Coulee. He has seen men
carry bodies to be burned at Galveston.
He has seen a typical Irish Street in Cork.
D'cu is moving slowly through his garden.
His deaf-aid whistles to the birds in flight.

Girl

I will worry for the world that has you in it now,
girl – the way you rose from me like dawn
from the hills, over the breeze-veined water.
It had no warning – no blood moon, no portents,
no earthquakes at your quickening but here
you are, tethering the sky with kite-strings, shouting
clouds into the frozen garden or pinning
down the bay with hands and knees
to interrogate the sand.
You leave shadows
crawling across the valleys of your footprints
and scorch the wind with the fire of your hair.
Even in your absence, a weak sun drifts,
window-shaped across your bed
and a pied cackle
pica pica
rattles down the chimney.

Oh the theft of you.

Nothing is certain or safe now, girl,
between here and the water,
my natural disaster,
my catastrophe, my daughter.

Not yet

I'm packing up the summer clothes again,
while outside there's a big sky piled
with clouds hay-waining by,
almost saying *it's not over*
just yet − wait a while
but in the chimney breast,
I hear the jackdaw fledglings' clatter
and the spiders crouching in the window-sill
cracks are getting fatter and the house is filled
with a stale chill like cold tea in a pot.
I'm trying not to see it as defeat −
the packing is as practical
as vacuuming the dust
that was once the tiny scales
of browned skin on warm, bare arms and legs.
The girl comes up the stairs
and catches me bagging up her best
summer dress.
She wants to wear it now. She must.
I look out of the window
to the cloudy threat, but already
she's elbowed her way out of her sweater.
So, laughing and trailing cheap silk,
she runs into the garden;
in the last beating
of summer rain, undefeated.

Carrying

The grandfather carries the boy
from the sea: little man slung
on the hip of a man. Those
could be the voices of elders
or wind, or waves,
curling into the shell of his ear.
Little man swayed over the shingle,
over the grey grass and singing –
but this is not the brown boy
with the blackcurrant eyes,
with the slow gaze,
who remembered every song –
pitch perfect,
the black of his pupils
grown large with the dark that empties into them.
Come hillock, come tussock, the grandfather carries
this boy, now, before the sun is at its height
and the adder, roused, strikes,
turns this boy to wax.
Because new love is like forgiveness,
not freely given but wrested
for want of words,
and the sun, humbling at noon,
with the tumble of waves and wind
behind him like so many fathers' voices
he carries the boy,
carries the man, carries the man.

Waiting

She is one who waits at windows –
one of few for whom
the passing traffic's tune
can tell the hour
more subtly than the hands
around a face:
the early morning's leavings,
the hush at ten, and how the bass
note of the 23 vibrates
the glass at noon.
She is one who waits and watches –
one who notices the changes
in the light
and in the starlings
burbling in the leaning rowan
against the purple sky, or after rain,
their shoaling flight.
She is one who lives by moments
of unknowing, in the gently dimming evening –
one who fills
the empty spaces with embellishments
and guesses, as the streetlamps
drop soft shadows on the road,
now quiet and still.
She is one who can remember
that the life before the watching
and the waiting at the window
was her own:
the wind on water, the voices
doused with laughter, on nights of noise and colour,
the touch of hands and faces;
from the sigh of shifting pebbles,
to the soft embrace of silence
in the moment before dawn.

Leaves

It's always you, walking away
down a lane edged with crowds of small,
quiet apples;
always you,
watched from a doorframe,
where wasps, heavy-winged with rain
and drunk on their last hours,
crawl and drop
from their parcel-paper lantern.
It's always your back receding
into slanting mist and turning leaves
and it will always be ended
with my submersion
into the warm lemon
of the noisy, soapsud house
– yellow with electric light and babies – always
I, who has to go on living, again
and again.